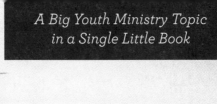
A Big Youth Ministry Topic
in a Single Little Book

THE SKINNY

ON

DISCIPLESHIP

Katie Edwards

with Ken Castor

Group

JESUS-CENTERED

Guide your entire ministry toward a passionate Jesus-centered focus with this series of innovative resources. Harness the power of these dynamic tools that will help you draw teenagers and leaders into a closer orbit around Jesus.

The Skinny on Discipleship
© 2015 Katie Edwards

group.com
simplyyouthministry.com

Credits
Authors: Katie Edwards with Ken Castor
Executive Developer: Tim Gilmour
Executive Editor: Rick Lawrence
Chief Creative Officer: Joani Schultz
Editor: Rob Cunningham
Art Director and Cover Art: Veronica Preston
Cover Photography: Rodney Stewart
Production: Joyce Douglas
Project Manager: Stephanie Krajec

Unless otherwise indicated, Scripture quotations are taken from the Holy Bible, New Living Translation, copyright ©1996, 2004, 2007, 2013 by Tyndale House Foundation. Used by permission of Tyndale House Publishers, Inc., Carol Stream, Illinois 60188. All rights reserved.

Scripture quotations marked NIV are taken from THE HOLY BIBLE, NEW INTERNATIONAL VERSION®, NIV® Copyright © 1973, 1978, 1984, 2011 by Biblica, Inc.™ Used by permission. All rights reserved worldwide.

ISBN 978-1-4707-2084-1
10 9 8 7 6 5 4 3 2   21 20 19 18 17 16

Printed in the United States of America.

ACKNOWLEDGMENTS

For Kurt Johnston—The reason I could write the pages of this book is because you modeled every word. Thank you for being my friend, my mentor, and the most influential leader in my ministry. Thank you for believing in me beyond what I believe possible for myself. And thank you for constantly challenging me to have faith and leap.

For Stacey Farr—Thank you for pouring over the pages of this book with me. Your wisdom, discernment, and deep love for students shaped me and shaped these pages. You are my dear friend and fan, and for that I am so grateful.

For Megan Bagnall, Darren Delin, Matt Heer, Bryce Kelley, and Josh Griffin—Thank you for being examples of Proverbs 27:17 in my life. The way you passionately love Jesus and deeply love students sharpens me more than you know. Grateful I get to learn from you and serve daily with you.

For Ron, Abby, Ella, and Cooper—Wife and mom are my very favorite roles to play. Thank you for loving me so deeply and creating space for me to be who God created me to be—because loving and creating that space for you is life's greatest joy for me.

— **Katie Edwards**

THE SKINNY

ON

DISCIPLESHIP

CONTENTS

THE SKINNY

ON

DISCIPLESHIP

The book you're holding might be "skinny," but that's because it's all-muscle. This means that Katie Edwards and Ken Castor have cut away the fat and focused on the "first things" that make discipleship in youth ministry powerful and long-lasting. In our Skinny Books series, we've paired a thought leader (in this case, Katie Edwards) with a master practitioner (in this case, Ken Castor) as a one-two punch. We want you to be challenged and equipped in both your thinking and your doing.

And, as a bonus, we've added an Introduction written by Duffy Robbins that explores discipleship through the filter of a Jesus-centered approach to ministry. Jesus-centered is much more than a catchphrase to us—it's a passionate and transformative approach to life and ministry. Duffy's Introduction to discipleship first appeared in my book *Jesus-Centered Youth Ministry,* and we couldn't think of a better way to kick off this little book. It's time to get skinny...

—RICK LAWRENCE
Executive Editor of Group Magazine

THE SKINNY

ON

DISCIPLESHIP

INTRODUCTION

I'd been scheduled to speak at a large denominational event out West, and about two weeks before the event I received a phone call from a woman on the "design team" who wanted to review with me some basic details of the conference. All in all, it was pretty a routine conversation. But then she added, without any hint of irony, this additional word of direction: "Please, when you give your talks to the kids, we've decided as a design team to ask that you not mention the name of Jesus. We don't mind if you talk about God; in fact, we hope you will. But we hope you'll understand that talking about Jesus will offend some of our young people, and we don't want to do anything that will make them feel uncomfortable."

I tried to imagine a traffic cop who couldn't bring himself to ask the driver to please keep his truck off of the sidewalk because he didn't want the driver to think he was unfriendly. Please understand that I'm entirely sympathetic with the motives that led these good folks to "design" the Designer out of their youth event. After all, they wanted to make the conference a safe place for kids to ask questions and feel accepted and comfortable. I agree with that. But just because we want all patients—

no matter how sick—to feel welcomed into the hospital, that doesn't mean that we hold back on the cure because we're afraid of offending the virus.

Several years ago I heard that the archbishop of Canterbury said the Church of England was "dying of good taste." I hope it's not in poor taste to say so, but I fear the same may be happening to us in youth ministry. I think a lot of us have come to terms with the scary parts of our work: unruly kids, unhappy parents, bad food, lock-ins, church vehicles, the church board. Sure, it's a storm, but we know these waters. What makes some of us uneasy is when Jesus shows up, walking on top of those storm-tossed waves.

I never agreed in that phone call to refrain from talking about Jesus. I couldn't. First of all, that's not me. And second, that's not the gospel. I *did* do the event, and I *did* talk about Jesus (a little more than normal). And what we all experienced that weekend, once again, was Jesus Christ meeting the desperate yearnings of kids restless and helpless in their adolescent storms.

—Duffy Robbins
Professor of Youth Ministry, Eastern University

CHAPTER 1

What

Is

Discipleship?

THE SKINNY

ON

DISCIPLESHIP

I started following Jesus at a summer camp when I was 14. I came home from that camp on fire for Jesus. But all I knew of what it meant to follow Jesus was what I learned there at camp. I had no idea where to go from that first step I had taken. And for a while I stayed in that same "camp high" place.

Until I met a leader in our youth group named Marcy. We became friends, and I started spending time with her after church on Sundays. One week I remember her asking me about my new friendship with Jesus. My response was "I think it's great." She said, "You think?" The truth was that I had no idea how my relationship with Jesus was. I just knew that I had placed my trust in him. But beyond that, I had no idea what it meant to *follow* him.

At the end of that conversation, Marcy invited me to be a part of a weekly small group Bible study at her house. I didn't know it at the time, but this was a life-changing invitation for me. I knew I loved Jesus and wanted to follow him, but I had no idea how. This small group became the place where I began learning about the "how." Through intentional relationships, time, and teaching I had my first exposure to praying, reading and studying God's Word, learning alongside other followers of Jesus, and discovering how to take everything I was learning and live it out. Like I said, it was life-changing.

Marcy provided a safe place for me to ask questions and wonder and doubt. She was a patient teacher who gently nudged me toward next levels in my faith in Jesus. She started discipling me when I was 14, and she walked alongside me until I was 25.

Every teenager needs a Marcy.

Really, every human needs a Marcy.

I truly believe that every teenager needs someone who is intentionally walking with them through a discipleship process—someone who is helping them grow as a disciple of Jesus Christ. If you are reading this, it looks like that someone could be you—even if your name isn't Marcy!

Let's talk about this word *discipleship*. What is it? There are many interpretations of the "who, why, when, what, and how" of discipleship. I asked three youth workers for their definition of discipleship, and while they have similarities, they're all a little different.

"Discipleship is building a relationship with a student, walking alongside them through the good and bad, and living a life of example for them to learn from."

Bryce, SMALL GROUP LEADER

"Discipleship is the action of assisting our students to become more like Christ, promoting ownership of their faith and genuine relationship with Jesus."

Emma, College Student/Youth Ministry Major

"Discipleship is modeled not taught from the stage."

Darren, Youth Pastor

In my opinion, these are all great, accurate statements about discipleship. But for our time together in this book, I want to break it down and simplify it even more.

I believe that in youth ministry we need a little bit of a broader stroke. No two teenagers are alike. Sure, we can find similarities among our students, but each young person experiences an individual, personal relationship with Jesus. Getting too specific with a definition can limit what we can do as disciplers in their lives. So I am going to offer the simplest definition of discipleship as we examine this issue together:

Discipleship: helping teenagers become like Jesus

Too simple? Perhaps. But think about this definition for a moment. You can attach this statement to any part of the discipleship process with any teenager you are working with:

- Helping teenagers become like Jesus through beginning a personal relationship with him

- Helping teenagers become like Jesus through reading and studying the Bible

- Helping teenagers become like Jesus through experiences that expand their faith and trust in him

- Helping teenagers become like Jesus through serving and being the church

- Helping teenagers become like Jesus through living out the Beatitudes

- Helping teenagers become like Jesus through letting the Fruit of the Spirit grow in their lives

- Helping teenagers become like Jesus through an intentional relationship with a Christ-like mentor

- Helping teenagers become like Jesus through modeling a devoted, passionate relationship with him

- Helping teenagers become like Jesus through helping them wrestle with their doubts about their faith

The simplicity of Katie's definition of discipleship is both profound and practical. In any particular moment the goal is to help teenagers become like Jesus in whatever step that person needs to take. By completing this statement in a number of ways, we are able to intentionally contextualize the discipleship process. Here are some more ideas:

- *asking them open-ended questions about their future*

- *taking them on a hiking adventure that serves as an analogy of their walk with God*

- *giving them significant, outrageous opportunities to serve others*

- *praying for them every day*

- *embedding Scripture in their minds*

While keeping in mind the teenagers that you know, take a moment to list at least five more ways that you could complete this statement "helping teenagers become like Jesus through...."

This list could go on for a while, so I'll stop here. This simple statement gives us the freedom to meet individual teenagers where they are and help them become like

Jesus. Through relationship, time, teaching, and next steps, we can be a part of the journey of helping our students become devoted disciples of Jesus Christ.

Now that we have established a working definition for discipleship, there is one more question we need to answer before we move forward: Why is discipleship so important? It's critical to answer this question because of the weight that this process carries. Jesus models discipleship throughout the Gospels. Jesus walked ordinary people through an intentional process to help them become his devoted disciples who would carry out his mission. A passage I am going to visit a few times throughout this book is Matthew 28:18-20. It's a bold command from Jesus, and it paints an incredible picture of the discipleship process:

> "Jesus came and told his disciples, 'I have been given all authority in heaven and on earth. Therefore, go and make disciples of all the nations, baptizing them in the name of the Father and the Son and the Holy Spirit. Teach these new disciples to obey all the commands I have given you. And be sure of this: I am with you always, even to the end of the age.' "

There is nothing accidental or unintentional or random about Jesus' relationship with the disciples. He spent time with them, he shared life with them, he taught them to obey, he shared experiences with them, he gave them direction, and he promised to be with them through every moment until the end of the age. This is the picture of what you and I are called to—this is the model for us to follow. And when we commit to this process with teenagers, we are fulfilling what Jesus asks us to do as his disciples.

My hope is that this simple book will encourage you and will become a practical guide as you move forward in your role as a disciple-maker. Understand that there are no shortcuts, there is no handbook for teenagers, and there is no timeline on what it will take to help each teenager become more like Jesus.

Follow the model of Jesus, rely on the fact that he is with you until the end of the age, and remember that ultimately he loves the teenagers you are working with even more than you do.

THE SKINNY

ON

DISCIPLESHIP

CHAPTER 2

Preparing

Our Hearts to

Disciple

Students

THE SKINNY

ON

DISCIPLESHIP

Before we can be intentional about the discipleship process with teenagers, we need to be intentional about our own heartbeat for Jesus. Helping students know Jesus on a deeper level requires that our own love for him and devotion to him run deep. It is impossible for us to be effective without first being connected to him. **Jesus needs to be the source from which we draw our strength, our wisdom, our unconditional love, and our discernment.**

❯ A LEADER'S PERSPECTIVE *Ken Castor*

Some people find it energizing to be in the presence of teenagers. Others feel absolutely drained after a night at youth group or a bus trip to the retreat. All the energy, all the passion, all the noise, all the moods, all the varying degrees of development and maturity—teenagers can exhilarate and exhaust. So it is essential that we find ourselves rooted deeply into Christ. We want our own lives to be standing in the strength of Jesus, ready for all the aspects of life that will come our way. Before encountering the exuberance of student activities, try these two simple ideas:

1. *PRAY that God will give you everything you need to be just what the students will need. Don't rely on your own strength; rely on Jesus.*

2. *PRAY that God will guide teenagers toward a devotion and commitment to growing down in Jesus. Whatever that next step into relationship with God may be, pray that they will take it.*

So, what are some things we can do to prepare ourselves for the discipleship process with teenagers?

SPEND TIME WITH JESUS

I realize this feels like a "no-brainer" statement. But honestly, there are times when we as youth workers can spend so much time "doing" ministry for Jesus that we forget to "be" his person first. Even the most experienced and educated youth workers fall into this trap.

Before you minister to the teenagers in your ministry, spend time with Jesus. Commit yourself to daily time talking with him, praising him, confessing to him, and reading your Bible. In John 15:4 Jesus says, "Remain in me, and I will remain in you." When we are connected to Jesus and looking to him, that is when we are going to be at our most effective in the discipleship process. *Are you spending consistent time with Jesus?*

CONTINUE THE PROCESS OF BECOMING LIKE JESUS

Our lives need to reflect the love of Jesus. We don't have to be perfect (because, of course, we *can't* be perfect), but we can be people who are faithfully on the journey of becoming like Jesus—this is what our students want and need to see. The last thing we want to do is give teenagers the impression that there is some sort of finish line in our walk with Jesus. I think the biggest thing I've realized about discipling young people is the value of being open about what God is teaching me personally. Once that trust and transparency are built, it is easier to pour into the life of a teenager.

Make sure you are taking the time to worship, be a part of the church, and fellowship with other followers of Jesus. Also make time for someone to be discipling you. You need encouragement and mentoring as much as your students do. *How are you becoming like Jesus?*

OPEN YOUR HEART TO BEING USED BY JESUS

Before you meet with the teenagers in your life, ask Jesus to use you. Ask him to help you be bold, be open, and love under any circumstance. This step of surrender and dependence opens up the door for Jesus to work through you in the discipleship process with your students. *What do you need to ask Jesus to help you do?*

Nurturing the condition of our heart is an ongoing process. Because we are "pouring out" during the process of discipling teenagers, we need to make sure that we are in the constant pursuit of being "poured into" by Jesus.

Here are three specific ways to spend time with Jesus:

- *Each day for six months, read one verse in Psalm 119. Repeat the verse again and again throughout the day, and let that one verse soak into you. The next day, move to the next verse and repeat the process.*

- *Intentionally meet with others who inspire you to grow closer to Jesus. In the exact same way that you hope to be an encouragement for teenagers, let someone speak into your life. If you were asked right now who those people would be, whose names would you mention? Why not reach out to those people right now and ask them to grab coffee with you?*

- *Stop being so busy. In other words, don't treat Jesus like something you need to add to your life. Make Jesus the center of your orbit, and measure the worth of everything else based on his presence at the core of your life. That means simplifying all the chaos around you. Then you will have "more" time for Jesus—and also for students.*

CHAPTER

3

Where

Do I

Begin?

THE SKINNY

ON

DISCIPLESHIP

"Jesus came and told his disciples, 'I have been given all authority in heaven and on earth. Therefore, go and make disciples of all the nations, baptizing them in the name of the Father and the Son and the Holy Spirit. Teach these new disciples to obey all the commands I have given you. And be sure of this: I am with you always, even to the end of the age.' "

— Matthew 28:18-20

"THEREFORE, GO AND MAKE...."

Wouldn't it be incredible if teenagers came to us and asked how to become more like Jesus? How great would it be if they pursued us, asked to start an intentional relationship, asked to read and study God's Word together, and asked to sit at our wise feet? Amazing, right?

I've been doing youth ministry for over 20 years, and I can count on one hand the number of times that has happened. Actually, I've never had a student ask to sit at my wise feet—just the other stuff. Most of the time, however, I'm chasing teenagers down and on a constant pursuit of helping them be more like Jesus. And as tough as that can be, I don't really think it's a bad thing. Think about it this way: When Jesus chose his 12 closest disciples, *he* pursued *them*. He had intentional conversations that invited them into the discipleship process.

I believe it's the same for those of us who serve as youth workers, whether we're full time or part time, vocational or volunteer. As we passionately pursue Jesus in our lives, we can invite students to be a part of the discipleship process with us. We need to be intentional about pursuing students and helping them become passionate followers of Jesus. As disciples, we are commanded to make disciples. So where do we begin in terms of reaching teenagers?

In Matthew 28:19 Jesus says, "Therefore, go and make disciples." Jesus' call to action assumes that *we* will be going to our teenagers. Jesus expects that we'll be seeking them out and pursuing a discipleship relationship with them. He anticipates that we'll be living our lives in such a way that we will intentionally help teenagers encounter the message of Jesus.

If we wait for them to initiate relationship or wait for them to come to us, we might be waiting awhile! It's not that teenagers don't want to be discipled; it's just that they might not fully understand what that means. It's up to us as leaders to lead, define, and invite.

There a few ways I believe we can be sure that we are "going" to teenagers.

*The Great Commission of Matthew 28:19-20 imitates the
Great Shema of Deuteronomy 6:4-9. "Hear this!" the Lord
instructed the Israelites. In essence God said: "You should
love me and you should help young people to love me. So as
you are going about your lives, intentionally help the next
generation to obey and follow me. As you eat, as you walk, as
you travel to work, as you talk with neighbors, as you pray
at night, as you use your hands and your brain, as you invite
teenagers into your home, let your life be so saturated by my
patterns that the next generation will pick them up, too!"*

PRAY FOR GUIDANCE

Who does Jesus want you to be intentional with? Ask
him. Have you ever asked him to reveal a specific student
to you? Try it. See what happens. Pray, "Jesus, bring me
the teenager that YOU want me to pour into and to help
passionately follow you." Then follow his lead and be
open to the person he leads you to.

Our tendency as youth workers is to want to be in control
of who we disciple, but there are times when Jesus has
something different in mind. And instead of choosing a
super-shiny, popular youth group kid, open your heart to
the teenager Jesus chooses for you. (He may guide you

toward more than one student, but in the following pages we'll talk about the process through a one-student lens.)

INITIATE THE CONVERSATION

Once you identify the teenager that Jesus is leading you to disciple, have an invitation conversation. Because students are rarely banging down our doors to be discipled, this might seem like it'll be an awkward encounter. But here's an important truth: Teenagers love to be invited. So trust Jesus, be bold, and start with one of these opening lines:

- "Hey, I've been praying, and Jesus has put your name on my heart. I would love to spend some intentional time with you to..."

- "Hey, I've noticed that you seem to be really passionate about following Jesus; I would love to be a part of your journey by..."

- "Hey, I think it's awesome that you placed your trust in Jesus at summer camp. I would love to come alongside you and help you become like Jesus through..."

- "Hey, I know you aren't really honoring Jesus with your choices right now, but I would love to help you find your way back to him. Are you open to meeting with me once a week to..."

Or if none of those openers feels natural to you, come up with your own—these are just a few basic lines to get you thinking. And don't ask me why I think it's good to start every conversation with "Hey"—it just feels right to me. Simply be intentional about inviting students into a discipleship relationship with you. Be the one to GO and TALK to a teenager.

⊙ A LEADER'S PERSPECTIVE Ken Castor

One great way to have an intentional conversation with teenagers is by helping them discover who they are through open-ended questions that reveal what God is doing in their life. Try starting conversations with the following questions, and just keep asking more questions that lead to a positive direction. And try your hardest not to offer answers. Trust your students to explore and to begin articulating God's work in their lives.

- *How would you define true success for your life?*

- *What are the three things in life that give your soul the deepest sense of fulfillment?*

- *What do you enjoy about your favorite activity?*

- *Think about the people who have made the biggest positive impact on your life—what did they say or do that changed you so much?*

MEET THEM WHERE THEY ARE

When beginning to disciple teenagers it can be easy to start where we as youth workers think we should start. We desperately want to share and impart our wisdom, but if we aren't careful we will put young people on our trajectory with Jesus instead of on their own trajectory with him. Yes, you are leading them on an intentional journey toward a deeper relationship with Jesus, but it's only going to work if you start at the right place.

The goal isn't to make teenagers become like you. The goal is to help them become like Jesus. Start in an honest place and help them take authentic, intentional steps in their relationship with Jesus. You can do this more effectively if you ask yourself some assessing questions about this teenager.

Here are some examples:

- What is this teenager's life like? How strong or weak are they relationships with their family? friends? other students in the youth ministry?

- Does this student genuinely know Jesus?

- Does this teenager go to church? enjoy being a part of the church?

- Does this student understand the message and good news of Jesus?

- Does this teenager have a Bible?

- Does this student regularly read the Bible? have an understanding of how to study Scripture?

- Does this teenager serve in any ministry? Has he or she expressed an interest in serving in some way?

Answer the questions through observation or just by asking your student. These and other "assessing" questions will give you insight on how to disciple this particular teenager. The answers will reveal where and how you can begin in the discipleship process.

Therefore, GO and PRAY for Jesus to reveal a specific teenager to you.

Therefore, GO and INVITE students into a discipleship relationship.

Therefore, GO and BEGIN where they are.

Therefore, GO and MAKE disciples.

→ A LEADER'S PERSPECTIVE *Ken Castor*

One of the most productive ways to GO and MAKE disciples is to get yourself invited to someone's house for a meal. Jesus arranged this very activity with Zacchaeus— and the tax collector's life was changed forever.

There is something amazing about sharing life together in someone's home. Walls are broken down, connection is established, trust is built, fears are diminished, and stereotypes are smashed. Once you have been invited into someone's home, have shared life and conversation, and have proven yourself to be a positive influence, families are much more likely to encourage your input in the life of their son or daughter.

As you're going about the routines of your life, you have to eat. And guess what? Teenagers and families need to eat, too! So set up opportunities to eat together!

CHAPTER 4

Making Disciples

THE SKINNY

ON

DISCIPLESHIP

If at this point you have any question about what your role in youth ministry is, this is it: making disciples and helping the teenagers in your youth group, your church, your school, and your community become like Jesus.

In order to begin "making disciples," we need to start with the source: Jesus.

During his time on earth, Jesus took a group of followers on an intentional journey with him. His mission was to develop these people into passionate, devoted disciples who would go and share the gospel in every corner of the earth.

Every lesson he taught, every moment he spent with them, every truth he shared, and every experience they had together led these disciples toward that mission. When we read the Gospels, we see that intentional journey unfold in a variety of ways.

Jesus was intentional with his disciples through...

- **RELATIONSHIPS.** When we first meet Jesus' disciples, we see relationships being formed with Jesus. He invites them into relationship with him.

- **TIME.** Jesus spent a great deal of time with his disciples. They traveled together, shared meals, and shared ministry experiences.

They listened to him teach, they saw him demonstrate compassion, and they watched him perform miracles.

- **TEACHING.** Jesus was constantly teaching his disciples about God's deep love for them (Luke 12:6-7), what it meant to follow him (Matthew 16:24-25), and what it meant to live for him (Matthew 5). Throughout the Gospels we find countless teaching moments between Jesus and his disciples.

- **NEXT STEPS.** Every moment that Jesus spent with the disciples was about moving them toward fulfilling his mission. In Matthew 28:19 Jesus gives his followers the ultimate next step: "Therefore, go and make disciples."

So how do we "make disciples"? We do it by taking our teenagers on an intentional journey to become like Jesus, live for him, place him at the center of their lives, and fulfill his purpose for them.

There are a variety of ways that we can help teenagers become like Jesus, but in this chapter I want to focus on the four specific areas that I just identified that Jesus modeled for us.

As we've already noted in Matthew 28:19, Jesus calls us to be "baptizing [people] in the name of the Father, the Son, and the Holy Spirit." The act of baptism is extremely important. Consider how you could make baptism in your church tradition a meaningful affirmation or rite of passage for teenagers. If students were christened early in life, what confirmation steps could you take to help that act take deeper root in their lives today? If they have never had the chance to be baptized, how could you use a baptism process to help them grow as followers of Jesus?

Helping teenagers live a "baptized" life is also crucial. Ultimately we want to see young people immersed in Jesus and rising to face everyday life with the resurrected power of Jesus. The analogy of baptism is a beautiful picture of what discipleship looks like.

WE MAKE DISCIPLES THROUGH RELATIONSHIPS

Helping Students Become Like Jesus Within a Mentoring Relationship

When I think of effective youth ministry, I think of the word *relationships*. I don't know of anything that teenagers value more or respond to better than this.

Solid, trusting relationships just have a way of unlocking teenagers' hearts in really cool ways.

Nick (not his real name) is a painfully shy 14-year-old student in my youth ministry. He is actively involved in our weekly program and loves being a part of our youth group, but he didn't start out that way.

The first week that Nick showed up to our ministry, he stood outside, face to the wall, unwilling to make eye contact or talk to anyone.

Literally, he was a wallflower.

I approached him and tried to coax him inside our program doors, but I couldn't get any kind of response from him. So I went to one of our leaders, Austin, and asked if he would stand with Nick and try to get him to come inside.

Austin started by just gently talking to the back of his head. Then I saw Nick turn around from the wall, and Austin was gently talking to his face. Then I saw Austin walk with Nick just inside our room and stand at the back wall.

And then finally Nick and Austin walked to the back row and sat together. As the service came to an end, I heard Austin say to Nick, "I'll see you next week!"

Asking others to join in the discipleship process is crucial. We often are limited in just how much we can singlehandedly do in the lives of young people. So grabbing other leaders and asking them for help must be a part of how we go about reaching others for Christ. We need to reject "lone ranger" mentalities of discipleship and embrace team-based approaches. Each person is gifted to effectively reach others in different ways.

Over the next few months Austin met Nick week after week, and I watched something lovely unfold. I saw what God could do through a relationship between a Christ-loving adult and a teenager. Over time Nick has become an active participant in our youth ministry. He is still painfully shy, but I have seen him soften and open up in such an awesome way—thanks to Austin's ongoing involvement and investment in his life.

I've seen Nick volunteer for gross games, join a small group, and sign up for some of our crazier events. I've seen him move from wallflower to an openhearted teenager all because of a friendship, a connection, a relationship. And because of that friendship with Austin, Nick is hearing God's Word, he is part of a weekly Bible study, and he is experiencing fellowship within the church. I believe that one little bit at a time, that relationship is nudging him to become like Jesus.

The discipleship process begins with solid, trusting relationships. **I would go as far as to say that relationships are *the key* in helping students become more like Jesus.** So where do we begin the process of building connections with young people? What elements are crucial to deepening our relationships with teenagers?

The ideas that I'm about to share are building blocks of great relationships with teenagers. They are not revolutionary, but when these simple elements are done intentionally, your connection with a teenager will get stronger—and ultimately you will see his or her relationship with Jesus go to the next level.

Show up. This sounds like a no-brainer, but great relationships require us to be consistent and "show up" in the lives of our students. It's simple: The more often you see each other, the more opportunities you will have to deepen your friendship. Great friendships are based on a consistent presence in each other's lives.

Ask good questions and then listen to the answers. The way that we are known within relationships is by asking great questions and listening to the answers. Ask your students great questions—the ones that are insightful, personal, open-ended, and can't be answered with just a yes or a no. And then hang on their every word as they respond. Great connections are based on being "known" by one another.

Make memories and laugh together. If you think of the deepest friendships in your life, it's almost a guarantee that you have had some fun moments together. It's incredible how laughter, inside jokes, and crazy memories can relax and open up a student's heart to a deeper connection. Some of my stronger friendships with teenagers began with an inside joke. Great relationships have fun at the foundation.

Be vulnerable and share. When we are building our connections with students, we sometimes get so caught up in getting them to open up that we forget about showing them pieces of ourselves. Great relationships require both sides to share, be vulnerable about strengths/weaknesses, and open up. Your willingness to share (appropriately, of course) shows a teenager that you are in process and on the journey of becoming like Jesus as well. Great friendships are built on people journeying together.

These are just four specific ways to build your connections with teenagers. There are so many more that will fuel and energize your discipleship journey with students.

Discipleship is much more of a process than a product. Growing the faith of teenagers involves multiple factors and multiple inputs throughout multiple development stages of their lives. "Spiritual" life is not separated from a teenager's physical, cognitive, emotional, or social growth. With this in mind, how could you help students grow closer to God as they grow through the process of their own personal development?

PHYSICAL: A teenager's body is going through major upheaval and change. How can helping them grow physically healthy enable them to grow spiritually healthy?

COGNITIVE: A teenager's brain is a lot more dynamic than yours! It is firing with more activity than at any other time of life except for infancy. How can you engage a teenager's brain in the process of learning about God?

EMOTIONAL: A teenager's heart is on a roller-coaster ride! In your time together, how can you involve their passions—their struggles, their joys, their fears, their confidence, their worries—in the process of learning about God?

SOCIAL: A teenager's friends are instrumental to their identity formation. In your time together, how can you value their friendships, encourage thoughtful reflection, and empower them to become disciple-makers themselves?

WE MAKE DISCIPLES WITH TIME

Helping Students Become Like Jesus Over Time

"Because we loved you so much, we were delighted to share with you not only the gospel of God but our lives as well" (1 Thessalonians 2:8, NIV).

When I think of the word *discipleship*, I immediately think of two other words: *process* and *time*. When helping students become like Jesus, you are entering into an intentional process that will unfold over time.

There are a few things about time that are important for you to understand. The first thing is that the time you spend with teenagers is crucial to the discipleship process. Nothing compares with time together.

The second thing I want you to understand about time is that you have enough of it. It might not feel that way, but you do. With a little creativity, you might be surprised where and when great discipleship can take place.

And lastly, I want you to understand that this discipleship journey with your teenagers may go beyond the time frame you've committed to initially. You might be starting the discipleship process with a freshman in high school, but this relationship could go beyond high school into college—or even into adulthood.

You may think you signed up to focus on only a particular window of a teenager's life, but your influence on that student's life can have generational impact. Psalm 78:1-7 says that when we disciple young people with the truths of God, they will in turn disciple those who come after them, who will in turn disciple those who aren't even born yet, who will then disciple those who really aren't even born yet. What you invest in the life of a young person today will impact many people for generations to come.

I started discipling Allison when she was 11—that was 21 years ago. I met her when she was entering junior high, and I know her today as a worship pastor at her church. In the last 21 years I have experienced countless seasons with her. Middle school seasons of discovering Jesus and asking tons of questions. High school seasons of navigating boys, navigating life as a Christian, and preparing for college. College seasons of contemplating what to do with her life. And then seasons well into adulthood.

We have had seasons when we have spent loads of time together, and there have been seasons when we have relied on social media to stay connected. There have been joyful moments, tough moments, disagreements, and some serious breakthroughs.

But most of all there has been time. Over time we have built a solid relationship, with multiple opportunities for me to nudge Allison toward becoming like Jesus. I am so grateful that the discipleship process did not end after middle school—we were just getting started at that point.

The journey with Jesus looks different for each of us and takes different levels of time and investment. As a youth worker we can feel this enormous pressure to "get things done" in the short time we have with teenagers. But why do we feel as if time is short? Time is what we make it. And if we think about intentionally discipling students over time, we have all of the time we need. I know that sounds idealistic—and yes, I believe that time is precious. But what if we spent loads of time with teenagers in some creative contexts? What if we made the most of the time we had our teenagers? What if we allowed every moment to help them become like Jesus and help see what it means to place him at the center of their lives? And what if we committed to helping students draw closer and closer to Jesus over time?

How can we make the most of our time with teenagers?

You can still be yourself while discipling students. You don't have to quit your life to be a good discipler. You can be an effective minister within the context of your time, your life, and your schedule. I'm a human who loves Jesus, I'm a wife, I'm a mom of three, and I'm a full-time youth pastor. You could say I have some stuff going on. And guess what? I have time to disciple students. I have a few students in different stages of life that I am intentionally discipling. But I am doing it in the context of my life and my time. That means I often have students at my dinner table, in my car, in my office, at my youth events—basically in every corner of my life.

Yes, I have margin. I take a day off. But in almost all of the other moments, I have students along for the ride. Discipleship is not a neat and tidy process. It is inconvenient, it's messy, and sometimes it doesn't fit into the context of my schedule. But for the most part I can be myself and can be an intentional part of the discipleship process with my students.

Share life—real life. If the goal is to help students become like Jesus, then we need to spend time helping them navigate real life with Jesus. We do this by sharing life with our students—sharing our own relationship with Jesus and navigating the ups and downs of life together. Help young people see how Jesus is present in everything from the mundane to the exciting. Eat meals together, run errands, go to sporting events, go to the movies, go to church together, and find other ways to spend time together. This will create more opportunities for you to nudge and encourage them forward in their faith in Jesus.

Be a real example. Our students can gain so much insight into their own relationship with Jesus by watching us live out our faith. They can observe the way we love others, the way we are impatient in the Starbucks line, the way we love our families, the way we face temptation, and the way we cope when things are tough. My own faith has expanded by watching other passionate Christians follow Jesus in everyday life. I am pretty sure how I love my husband and the way I parent my own kids can be traced back to my small group leader in college. **Your students need real examples to follow. They don't need Christians who pretend to have it all together or who have all of the answers.** They just need time with the real you.

"Time" comes in many forms. There are days, weeks, and months that the discipleship process with a student will requires a lot of face-to-face time. But for long-term discipleship, I think there are many ways that we can continue to help people become like Jesus through different avenues than face-to-face time. Some examples:

• Time in prayer • Time encouraging through social media • Time texting a verse or an encouragement • Time planning an event together	• Time talking on the phone • Time leaving an intentional voice mail • Time sending them something specific to read

I realize this idea of time can feel overwhelming. You've signed up to be a small group leader once a week for the next school year, and here I am talking about a 21-year commitment! Don't freak out. I am merely suggesting that we don't need to cram a lifetime of discipleship in a two-, four-, or seven-year period of time. We can think about starting a process with our students that MAY go beyond where you are with them right now and that MAY bleed into all areas of your life at the most inconvenient times. But take it from me: The rewards are worth it!

WE MAKE DISCIPLES BY TEACHING

Helping Students Become Like Jesus Through Teaching

Teaching is essential to the discipleship process with teenagers. In our desire to help students become like Jesus, we need to be people in their lives who are willing to teach them how to do that. For some of you, this idea excites you—and for others, this idea terrifies you.

If you're excited to impart your incredible wisdom to all of the young people that God brings into your path, allow me to say this: SLOW DOWN. This is not about your education process; this is about the teenagers you are discipling. This is about where they are. This is about where they can learn and grow. And this is about you being a person that God uses to teach others.

If you're terrified at the thought of teaching teenagers, allow me to say this: BREATHE. No seriously, take a deep breath. This is not about how much you know or don't know. This is not about preaching to thousands. You don't have to be a Bible scholar or a preacher to be a great teacher. You just need to have the desire to meet students where they are and help them continue to grow in their understanding of their faith. Be a learner yourself and be comfortable with saying, "I don't know," and you will be just fine.

❯ A LEADER'S PERSPECTIVE Ken Castor

"Disciple" literally means "learner." So a "disciple" of Jesus is someone who is a "learner" of Jesus. Model for your students a life of learning in Jesus. Young people don't trust adults who act as if they have it all figured out. Teenagers gravitate toward authenticity of the journey—and so they want to walk with adults who are walking with them.

Where do we begin? And what do we teach? These are the kinds of tough questions we face as youth workers when it comes to discipleship. No matter how you react to the idea of teaching students, I want to give you a place to begin. There are countless lessons that you could walk through with your students. Again, I just want to give you a starting point and some basic areas to consider.

Teach them the message of Jesus. It's so important for teenagers to understand and articulate the good news of Jesus Christ. You cannot help students begin the process of becoming like Jesus if they do not have a basic understanding of the gospel. I say "basic" because I believe that as they grow in their love and relationship with Jesus, their understanding of the gospel will become richer and deeper. This is a great starting point for intentional teaching and conversation.

Teach them to be thirsty. I love these words from Jesus: "But whoever drinks the water I give them will never thirst. Indeed, the water I give them will become in them a spring of water welling up to eternal life" (John 4:14, NIV). Teach teenagers to study the Bible, teach them to memorize Scripture, teach them to desire to grow in their knowledge of Jesus, teach them to talk to Jesus, and teach them to pursue God's mission for their lives. Through questions, conversations, and intentional time together in God's Word, your students can develop a genuine "thirst" for Jesus in their lives.

Teach them to obey. This might be the easiest one to teach—but not the easiest for our teenagers to do. This also might be the one area of teaching where you will get the most frustrated with the students you are discipling.

The Bible is full of commands, instructions, and truths that lead us to the abundant life that God promises.

However, as humans we are in a constant battle to obey. As youth workers, we would love to believe that "obeying" is simple and easy. But obedience is difficult for even the most mature followers of Jesus. Take this area one step at a time. There are many places you can begin with teaching in this area, including Matthew 22:36-40 (the Great Commandment), Exodus 20 (the Ten Commandments), and John 15 (staying connected to the Vine). There is so much coaching and teaching that happens in the discipleship process—thank goodness we have the time, right?

⊙ A LEADER'S PERSPECTIVE *Ken Castor*

"Obey" literally means "listen." While many youth workers would love to get students to "listen" to them, ultimately our goal is that we would all be listening to Jesus. So in your time with teenagers, give them the opportunity and the tools they'll need to "listen" to him.

Give them chances in your small group time to ask Jesus questions and to seek his direction. Give them chances to follow through on God's commands, to love a neighbor through a thoughtful service project, to use encouraging words, and to provide an offering for those in need. Give them a chance to read the Bible and to articulate what God is saying (rather than telling them what God is saying).

Teach them to live. How do we teach a teenager to live like and live for Jesus? I really don't know any better place to start than the Beatitudes. The words of Jesus himself give us a play-by-play of what it looks like to follow God with our lives. Spend time walking students through Matthew 5:1-12 to discover the life that we are called to lead. This is definitely not a one-time lesson. As students get older and enter new seasons of life, continue to revisit this passage. The way we tend to live out this passage changes over time.

◉▸ A LEADER'S PERSPECTIVE *Ken Castor*

Encourage students to share their personal stories of faith over and over and over and over again. The idea is not that they'll memorize a "perfect" testimony but that they'll become more aware of the ways Jesus has worked in their lives and more aware of how that reality can encourage others. Here are some ideas to help teenagers articulate their own testimony in a way that can be brief and Jesus-centered:

- *Encourage students to write down how Jesus grabbed ahold of them*

- *Encourage students to write down how Jesus is active in their lives today*

- *Encourage students to write down what Jesus is calling them to do for him in the years ahead*

Teach them to fish. Read Matthew 4:19 and inspire your students to discover "how to fish for people." Spend time teaching them how to share the message of Jesus with people they know and with people they don't know. Teach them to live according to Matthew 5:13-16 and be the salt of the earth and the light of the world.

This can be a scary and difficult thing for teens to wrap their minds around, so be patient but bold in teaching why this is an important part of our mission as Christ-followers. Again, this is not a one-time lesson. Teenagers' circle of influence will change as they get older. Encourage them to "fish" no matter what pond they live in.

Look for teaching moments. As you deepen your relationship and share life with your students, you will witness multiple teaching opportunities present themselves. They might come in the most unlikely moments, so keep your eyes and ears open.

For example, I was driving with a student the other day and she told me about some trouble she was having with one of her friends. It was a casual conversation in the car, but it gave me the chance to point her toward trusting Jesus and reading Scripture. And then I encouraged her to pray specifically about the situation. I realize that doesn't sound like hard-core teaching, but for a freshman in high school it was just the teaching she needed. There are little moments that can turn into big opportunities.

Many of Jesus' most memorable words and events arose out of spontaneous moments. He taught about judgment when a woman was caught in adultery (John 8:1-11); he helped people understand faith when a centurion approached him for help (Matthew 8:5-13); he turned an argument into a reflection about heaven (Matthew 18:1-7); he revealed his authority when some guys tore apart the building he was already teaching in (Mark 2:1-12); and he used a kid's basket of food and the hunger of a crowd to demonstrate God's provision for his people (Matthew 14:13-21). To teach like this ourselves, we must remain in an attitude of readiness. Our spiritual reflexes must be primed and ready to capture these moments as they occur.

Teach in various settings. Jesus taught in a host of different settings and through many different experiences. When you're teaching teenagers, think about ways to teach God's Word through a tangible experience. Give them ways to live out the life that Jesus is calling them to lead.

Teach them James 2 and then give them an opportunity to live it out. Teach them Matthew 6:14 and then give them an opportunity to live it out. Teach them 1 John 1:5-10 and then give them the opportunity to live it out. **Teach them to live for Jesus.**

Car rides often create some amazing spontaneous teachable moments. Here are some ways to encourage and capitalize on those moments:

- *Turn on the radio to a popular music station and have a conversation about culture.*

- *Ask everyone in the car to respond to questions that are deep but surprisingly fun, such as: "If for some reason you were covered in fish guts and had to swim for 30 minutes in shark-infested waters, describe all the things you might say to God during that time."*

- *Discuss what the teenagers hope to get out of the destination. If you're going to a youth event, ask students an intentional question about how they'd like to be impacted or what they think God might want to do in their lives.*

Share your learnings. As you learn and grow in your own faith, share your learnings along the way with your students. All of us can learn so much from the journey that other Christ-followers are on. So share your milestones with Jesus—they can turn into great teaching moments for teenagers.

One constructive way to make room for doubt is to study the psalms. The psalms are filled with questions of faith. But they show that doubt can actually reveal a foundation of a trusting relationship in God.

For example, the question "Where are you, God?" reveals that a person believes that God should be present, particularly during difficult times. The question "Why are you letting this happen?" reveals that a person believes God should be protecting and providing. Doubt is our way to express the disorientation of our faith.

So if a teenager expresses doubt, don't shut down the doubt. Instead, surprise him or her by affirming how doubt evidences faith. Then discuss how part of the process of learning to follow Jesus involves wrestling with the questions of faith.

Dive into the psalms, read Jesus' prayer in the Garden of Gethsemane before his arrest (Matthew 26), or work through Elijah's frustrations following his spiritual mountaintop experience (1 Kings 19). Walk alongside teenagers during their moments of doubt.

Allow room for doubt and questions. Doubt might seem like a scary thing to encourage, but doubt is essential to helping teenagers grow in their understanding of what it means to place their faith and trust in Jesus. Encourage your students to "push back" and ask challenging questions. They likely will ask some questions that you won't be able to answer. That's okay. That's a good thing. Look for answers together. Teach them to seek God's Word or lean on others to find answers. Doubt can lead to an ownership of their faith.

Enjoy the journey of discovery that comes with teaching! It can be a fun and fulfilling experience with your students!

WE MAKE DISCIPLES BY ENCOURAGING NEXT STEPS

Every Teenager Has a Next Step Toward Becoming More Like Jesus

Malia is a student that I've been discipling over the past year. She loves Jesus and is in the beginning stages of following him. She has a genuine desire to expand her faith and grow deeper in her relationship with Jesus. When we spend time together, I'm intentional about giving her some next steps that can help her become like Jesus.

Even without instructions or those next steps that I provide, I believe Malia could eventually find her way toward significant growth. But there is something really special about intentional direction in the discipleship process.

When people who know us and love us take the time to point us toward Jesus and expand what we know and how we think about him, it can be really exciting—as a disciple *and* as a discipler.

There are so many ways that we can encourage this process of next steps with our students. Here are just a few for you to think about.

What's next? Every time you meet with a student that you're discipling, consider ending your time together by talking about what's next. Is it something the teenager needs to do? Is it something he or she needs to think about? Is it something he or she needs to seek out in the Bible? Is it something he or she needs to talk to God about? What's next?

This might be a question the teenager can answer on their own, or it might be a question that you help him or her answer. Either way, this question will undoubtedly lead toward growth.

Our next step is to become a master at letting young people state what they believe. In your experience with students, you've probably noticed that they don't like being told by adults what to do. Teenagers love the trailblazing process. So give them the tools to discover the path that Jesus has prepared for them, and then them give frequent opportunities to personally declare how he wants them to go forward. Encourage them to establish achievable goals, and be sure to follow up on whatever action plan they develop.

Speak truth and gently nudge. As we walk through the discipleship process with our students, we need to be willing to help them move to next levels in their faith. At times this process is simple—and at times this process is difficult. It's simple to nudge students toward growth when they are on fire for Jesus and eagerly desire to grow deeper in their faith. It's a whole different story when students don't want to see what you see or don't want to grow in the ways that they need to.

No matter where your student is, speak the truth in a loving way and talk about clear next steps in their walk with Jesus. If they need to forgive, or they are trapped in sin, or they are caught up in bitterness, spend time lovingly giving them direction that will benefit them. Always be honest, and always be loving. I really believe those two things can inspire teenagers who are passionate about following Jesus—and can unlock the hearts of teenagers who are resistant.

Help them see what they don't see right now. Have you ever been in a situation where you were trying to figure something out, and all along the answer had been staring you in the face? Have you ever thought about that in regards to your walk with Jesus—wondering what is next or where you can be stretched and then someone comes along with the simplest of steps for you to take? This happens to me often.

Many of our students want to grow in their faith, but they just can't see the next step. That is where you come in. Help them see the things they don't. Help them become like Jesus by providing simple, difficult, challenging, or stretching next steps for them. This might include talking to them about areas where they might be getting it wrong or where they are making unwise choices. It also could include discussing where they are getting it right and how to take those wise choices to the next level.

The bottom line is that every teenager you disciple has a next step in his or her relationship with Jesus,

just as we disciplers can continue growing deeper in our faith. I am grateful for the mentors in my life who have pushed me (gently and not so gently at times) toward next levels of growth in my faith in Jesus Christ. This part of the process can be difficult at times, but this is where we really start to see teenagers move toward becoming like Jesus.

As I stated at the top of this chapter, there are a variety of ways to be intentional in the discipleship process with your students. Don't limit yourself to just the topics that I've discussed. The overall point I want to drive home is that no matter what process you decide to take your teenagers through, start by being deliberate. Jesus' process with the disciples was thoughtful and intentional. My own small group leader took me on a journey that led me to becoming a devoted disciple of Jesus. As you seek to help teenagers become like Jesus and place him at the center of their lives, create an intentional path that you walk down together.

THE SKINNY

ON

DISCIPLESHIP

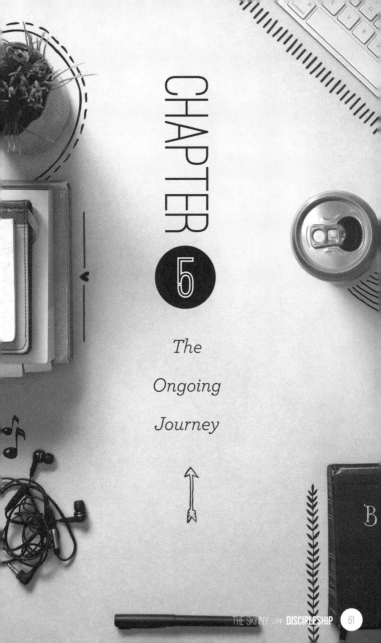

CHAPTER 5

The

Ongoing

Journey

THE SKINNY

ON

DISCIPLESHIP

The ongoing journey of discipleship with teenagers can be unpredictable, to say the least. But remember that this is a journey, not a race with a finish line. While here on this earth, we always have areas where we can grow and mature as followers of Jesus. As you embark on the discipleship process with a teenager, I want you to remember a few things.

DON'T SWEAT THE SMALL STUFF

At the end of the day, everything you are doing is discipleship. If teenagers are not responding the way that you want them to or are not moving at the pace that you hoped, it's okay—discipleship is still happening. The fact that you are intentionally caring for them is still an act of moving them toward becoming like Jesus.

EVERY TEENAGER IS ON A DIFFERENT PACE

When you start spending time with specific teenagers in your life, just keep your head down and stay focused on them. It is common among youth workers to compare where students are—and to feel discouraged when one of those students doesn't seem as "on track" as others might be. Remember that every teenager is on his or her own individual journey with Jesus—and that what truly matters is that each person is moving at just the right pace and consistently drawing closer to Jesus.

SOMETIMES TEENAGERS DON'T WANT TO BE DISCIPLED

You can begin the discipleship process with a student, but that doesn't mean you are going to finish it. I had a student a few years ago that I was discipling. When I started spending time with her, she loved Jesus, she was active in our youth group, and she was serving in our children's ministry. She was hungry for next steps with Jesus, and she was always up for any challenge I threw her way.

But when she entered her sophomore year of high school, she slowly started to pull away from me and from the church altogether. She began hanging out with a rough crowd of friends and started making some bad choices. I attempted to keep our relationship and her relationship with Jesus moving forward, but all of my efforts failed. And as much as I loved her, it wasn't enough. She needed to "want it," too. I continue to pray for her and keep the lines of communication open, but that is all I can do.

There are simply times when teenagers walk away from Jesus, and as much as we want to control or change that, we can't. I know this is kind of a downer—but I don't want you to feel discouraged by this. **Remember that Jesus loves every teenager in your youth ministry even more than you do!** Trust him to draw them back!

PARTNER WITH PARENTS

As much as our students don't want to admit this, their parents are still the most influential people in their lives. So it would only make sense to include parents in the discipleship process with teenagers. Without betraying any confidences, keep parents informed on what is happening with their child. As a parent of a teenager, I love when my daughter's small group leader informs me of the ways Abby is growing in her relationship with Jesus. I don't want to know everything that they discuss, but it's really cool when her leader shares stories or milestones in my daughter's life.

Don't be afraid to include parents, and don't be afraid to offer suggestions on things to discuss or work though with their child. For example, if you are studying the book of John with their teenager, let the parents know— and encourage them to read it, too. There are a lot of small things that you can do to open up conversation and discipleship between parents and teenagers. Remember: Parents are extremely important to the discipleship process. You really, truly want them to be involved.

➲ A LEADER'S PERSPECTIVE *Ken Castor*

I believe youth workers have the opportunity to equip parents to be the heroes. Some people sign up for youth work because teens need a hero, an advocate, or a champion. But some youth workers don't want to admit that parents really are the most influential people in the lives of teenagers.

The most effective way to increase the likelihood that teenagers will continue in faith as they grow older is if their parents walk alongside them in faith. So while we might run into our students a couple of hours a week (if we are lucky!), parents have dozens of hours each week to influence their son or daughter. Champion parents to become intentional disciple-makers for their kids. Parents don't need to be experts, just fellow learners.

In many ways, the ideas in this book can be implanted into the everyday relationship that parents are privileged to have with their teenagers.

IT'S OKAY TO INVEST IN A FEW

Jesus had 12 close disciples, but he invested in three of those guys on a deeper level. I am not saying that Jesus faced the same limitations as us, but he was intentional about going deeper with fewer than the 12. I don't know how many students you are caring for in your youth ministry setting, but it's okay for you to choose "a few" to invest in on a deeper level. You probably don't have the capacity to be intentional with more than just a few students. Multiply yourself by finding other leaders to join the process with you so every teenager in your youth ministry can be discipled personally.

TRY NOT TO GET FRUSTRATED

One of the most difficult things in the discipleship process is to watch our teenagers make mistakes or mess up. *If they would just listen to us, we could save them from so much pain and suffering!* Think about how Jesus felt when he saw his disciples make unwise choices or decisions or say things that revealed questionable motives. I wonder how many times Jesus thought to himself, "If they would *just listen to me.*" Keep your arms open wide, provide loving correction, offer forgiveness when it's needed, keep the lines of communication open, and then keep moving forward. Remember that discipleship is messy and unpredictable at times.

But discipleship is really fun when...

- A teenager has "aha" moments in his or her relationship with Jesus

- A teenager takes big risks for Jesus

- A teenager shares the message of Jesus with one of their friends

- A teenager gets excited about reading the Bible

- A teenager starts asking really good questions that you can't easily answer

- A teenager experiences life-change on a mission trip that you suggested

- A teenager becomes a discipler—because he or she wants to be like you

CHAPTER

6

Some

Final

Thoughts

THE SKINNY

ON

DISCIPLESHIP

I couldn't think of a better way to end this book than with a letter straight from my heart.

To my youth ministry friend,

We probably haven't met, but I want you to know that I believe in you. And I can believe that you are important in the mission of Jesus Christ.

I know that jumping into the discipleship process with teenagers might feel overwhelming. You might feel like you are not equipped, not educated enough, not old enough, not young enough, not cool enough, too busy, or just plain not ready. Here's what you need to know: You can do this. **As a devoted disciple of Jesus, you are equipped to play this important role.**

Over the years I've been a part of the discipleship process with many teenagers. Some of those individuals continue to love Jesus deeply and are devoted disciples, and some of them are still finding their way back to him. But no matter what the outcome has been of these relationships, I know that Jesus loves each person deeply and that he has a plan for them. He used me as a tool in their lives, and for that I am grateful. And I remain hopeful that every person I have had the privilege of working with would completely and passionately follow our Lord, Jesus Christ.

What I am trying to say is that this process is not about you—or success stories or positive outcomes. **The discipleship process is about us as disciples responding to Jesus' call to go and make disciples.** It's about opening our hearts completely to being used by Jesus. It's about us as disciplers being completely surrendered to Jesus in our own journey. And it's about allowing what Jesus is doing in us to overflow into all of the relationships around us.

Like I said, you can do this...*because he can do this.*

"Your love for one another will prove to the world that you are my disciples" (John 13:35).

You are loved....so go and love.

You are a disciple...so go and make disciples.

You are called...respond.